Learn to Code

Practice Book 1

Written by

Claire Lotriet

Published by

RISING ★ STARS

Rising Stars UK Ltd, part of Hodder Education, an Hachette UK Company, Carmelite House, 50 Victoria Embankment, London, EC4Y 0DZ
www.risingstars-uk.com

Every effort has been made to trace copyright holders and obtain their permission for the use of copyright materials. The author and publisher will gladly receive information enabling them to rectify any error or omission in subsequent editions.

All facts are correct at time of going to press. All referenced websites are correct at time of going to press.

The right of Claire Lotriet to be identified as the author of this work has been asserted by her in accordance with the Copyright, Design and Patents Act 1998.

Published 2015
Reprinted 2015, 2016
Text, design and layout © Rising Stars UK Ltd. 2015

Author: Claire Lotriet
Computing consultant: Miles Berry
Text design: Words and Pictures Ltd, London
Typesetting: Words and Pictures Ltd, London
Cover design: Burville-Riley Partnership
Publisher: Becca Law
Editorial: Jenny Draine
Project manager: Estelle Lloyd
Illustrations: Eva Sassin, Advocate Art

Photo acknowledgements: pages 8–10, 12–14, 16–18, 20–22: screenshots from Scratch http://scratch.mit.edu licensed under Creative Commons licence. Scratch is developed by the Lifelong Kindergarten Group at the MIT Media Lab; pages 24–26, 28–30, 32–34, 36–38: screenshots from *Microsoft* PowerPoint® used with permission from *Microsoft*®; pages 40–42, 44–46, 48–50, 52–54: screenshots from *Microsoft* Excel® used with permission from *Microsoft*®.

Rising Stars is grateful for the following people and their schools who contributed to the development of these materials: Matt Rogers, Snowsfields Primary School; Dawn Hallybone, Oakdale Junior School; Marc Faulder, Burton Joyce Primary School; Martyn Soulsby, North Lakes School; John Janowski, Royal Russell Junior School.

British Library Cataloguing in Publication Data.
A CIP record for this book is available from the British Library.

ISBN: 978-1-78339-341-1

Printed by Multivista Global Ltd, India.

Contents

How to use this book

Learning to code can seem like learning a new language! This book will show you how to code using three different tools. You will make your own games and animations!

The step-by-step instructions explain what you need to do.

8 Duplicate slide 5. Use the *Scribble* tool to extend the roots on slide 6. Now use the *Scribble* tool to add a green bud at the top of the stem. Can you predict what you will change in the next slide?

Each slide has to change slightly to create the animation sequence.

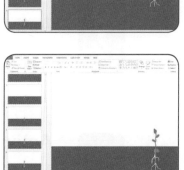

Handy tips give you extra help.

9 Duplicate slide 6. On slide 7, use the `Shape Fill` colour tool to change the bud to the petal colour you would like your flower to have.

The slides have to be in the right order for your animation to make sense.

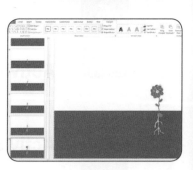

This text shows the commands you need to use in the program.

10 Duplicate slide 7. Copy and paste the flower bud several times on slide 8. Arrange the buds in a circle to create petals for your flower. Turn the petals to face different directions using the green circle tool. Add small yellow circles for the pollen. The sequence is now complete.

This text shows the words you'll see on the screen.

This text shows what you need to type in.

11 Click on the `Transitions` tab. Under *Advance Slide*, make sure the *After* box is ticked. Set at **00:03.00** and select `Apply To All`. Click on the `Slide Show` menu and then select `From Beginning` to watch your sequence play as an animation.

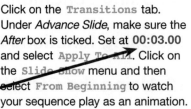

The pictures show what you should see on your screen.

This book uses three tools: Scratch, PowerPoint and Excel. Work your way through the activities for each tool in order. Each activity builds on the previous one.

Now try this . . .

- o Can you change the speed at which your animation plays using the *Transitions* tools?

- o Can you add some sky and clouds in the background and change them slightly on each slide so it looks like they are moving when your animation plays?

- o Can you create a similar animation for a different plant or flower?

- o Can you create a sequence of slides to animate two or more flowers growing?

- Draw a sequence of pictures that show the full life cycle of a plant. Mix them up and challenge a partner to put them in order. How did they know what order to put them in?

Take your learning further by trying these extra challenges!

These activities help you develop your understanding of coding away from the computer.

Key words

Can you explain to a partner what these words mean?

animation   **sequence**   **change**   **duplicate**   **order**

These are important words that you need to understand. You can find definitions in the glossary on page 56.

How did you do?

Think about what you did in this activity. Did you.

- o duplicate your slides to allow you to make changes to the sequence of your animation?

- o change the picture of the flower slightly each time?

- o copy and paste different parts of your picture?

- o sequence the different drawings correctly so your animation made sense?

- o change the slide show settings so your animation played continuously?

- o change the speed at which your animation played?

- o add changes to the background in your animation?

Use these questions to review what you have learned in the activity.

27

Writing code to make something happen is exciting, but sometimes your code won't work as well as it could, or it won't work at all!

What happens when your code doesn't do what you want it to? You need to fix it!

The process of making our code better, or correcting mistakes (removing bugs in the code) is called debugging.

If you find a problem with your code, try to solve it yourself first, before asking a grown-up. The coding monsters are here to help you!

When you have finished writing your code, always run your program or script to see if it works.

Go through your code step by step in your head. Try to predict what will happen. Can you spot any mistakes?

for coding

Try explaining each bit of your code to a partner. Does it all make sense?

Try explaining your code to a rubber duck. Rubber duck debugging is used by proper programmers to fix errors in their code!

Show your code to a partner. Do they have any ideas about how to fix code that isn't working?

Activity 1: Scratch Programming a sprite

Use Scratch at www.scratch.mit.edu. Click *Create* to start!

In this activity you will build a script for an animation of a bat. First you will make the bat move between two points on the screen, then you will make the bat talk and finally you will add a screaming sound effect!

1 Start by right-clicking on the cat 'sprite'. Click `delete` to remove the cat sprite (he is not needed for this animation).

> Scratch has a whole library of different characters (called sprites) to choose from.

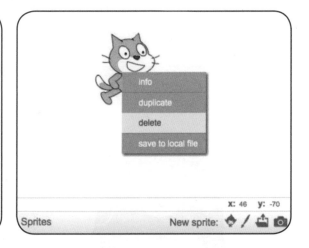

2 Now let's choose a sprite to animate. Click on the `Choose sprite from library` icon. Click on `Bat1` to select it and then click on `OK`. Bat1 should now be in your *Sprites* box.

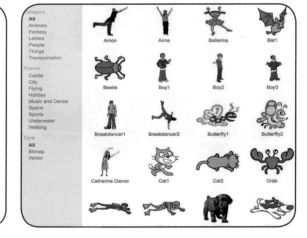

3 Click on the `Choose backdrop from library` icon in the bottom left corner of the screen to bring up the *Backdrop Library*. Click on `City` in the *Theme* menu on the left. Now click on `night city` to select it and then click on `OK`.

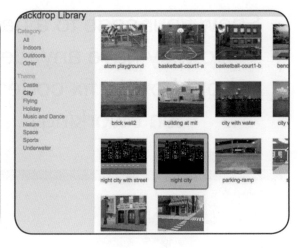

4

In the *Sprites* box, click on the `Bat1` sprite. Your sprite will appear in the grey scripts area on the right. Now click on the `Scripts` tab at the top. We will build a sequence of commands for the bat called a program. Click on `Events`. Drag the `when ⚑ clicked` block into the scripts area.

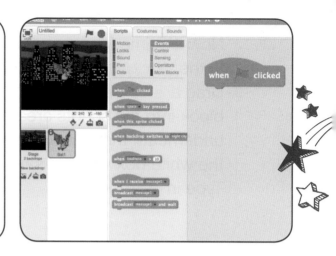

5

In the `Scripts` tab, click on `Motion`. Drag a `glide 1 secs to x: … y: …` block into the scripts area and place it underneath the `when ⚑ clicked` block so they 'snap' together.

The sprite will follow the commands in the sequence that you order the blocks in.

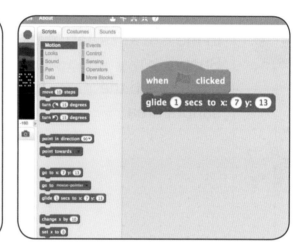

6

Click in the white `x` box and type in **140**. In the `y` box, type **80**.

These numbers show the position that the bat will glide to. The x-number shows the horizontal position and the y-number is the vertical position. These are called coordinates.

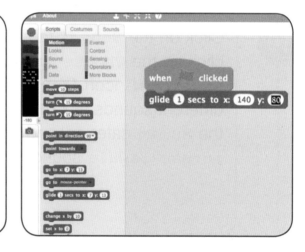

7

Drag another `glide…` block into the scripts area. Snap it underneath the first `glide…` block. Click in the white `x` box and type in **-140**. In the `y` box, type **-80**. Click on the `when ⚑ clicked` block to preview the bat moving between the two points.

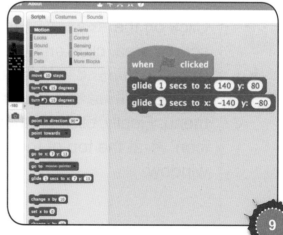

8

Now it's time for some sound effects. In the `Scripts` tab, click on `Looks`. Drag a `say Hello! for 2 secs` block into the scripts area and snap it underneath the `glide...` blocks. Click the white box where it says *Hello!*. Type in **Boo!** instead.

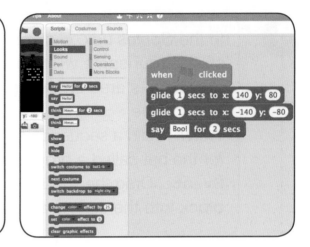

9

In the `Scripts` tab, click on `Sound`. Snap a `play sound pop` block underneath the `say...` block in the scripts area.

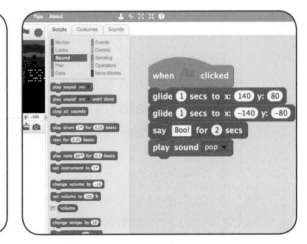

10

Click on the `Sounds` tab and then click on the `Choose sound from library` icon. (You can choose different sounds as output.) Click on the `Human` category and select the `scream-female` sound. Click on `OK`.

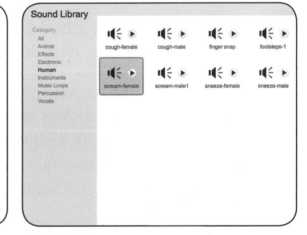

11

Click on the `Scripts` tab. In the scripts area, click on the arrow in the `play sound pop` block. Choose `scream-female` in the drop-down menu. Finally, click on the green flag icon ⚑ at the top of the preview window.

Now try this . . .

- Can you change what the bat says in the speech bubble?

- Can you change how quickly the bat moves between the two different places on screen?

- Can you change the sound effect at the end? Can you record your own?

- Can you add some more `glide...` blocks so the bat moves between four different points instead of two?

 Write a sequence of commands for a partner to move around the classroom as if they were a sprite.

Key words

Can you explain to a partner what these words mean?

command   **script**   **sprite**   **program**   **sequence**

How did you do?

Think about what you did in this activity. Did you:

- change the sprite to a bat and the backdrop to a night city scene to suit your animation?

- sequence the blocks in your script in the correct order so your animation worked?

- follow the steps to program the sprite to move between two points?

- change what the bat said by adjusting the `say...` block?

- change the `play sound...` block so a scream could be heard at the end?

Activity 2: Scratch
Programming a sprite using repetition

As well as programming a sprite to move, you can also use repeat blocks so a sprite moves continuously. In this activity you will build a script for an animation of an octopus who never stops swimming!

1

First, right-click on the cat and click on `delete`. Click on the `Choose sprite from library` 😈 icon and select `Octopus`. Click `OK`.

The octopus has two costumes. Costumes are different versions of the same sprite so they can have different looks.

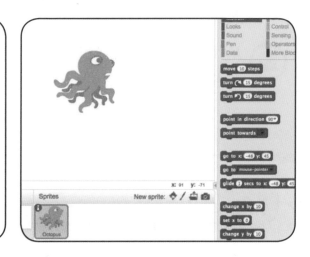

2

Click on the `Choose backdrop from library` 🖼 icon at the bottom left and click on the `Nature` theme. Select the `underwater2` backdrop and then click `OK`. Click on the octopus sprite in the *Sprites* box.

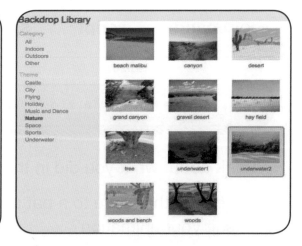

3

Click on the `Scripts` tab and then on `Events`. Drag a `when ▶ clicked` block into the scripts area. In the `Scripts` tab, click on `Control`. Drag and snap a `forever` block underneath.

Any command within the `forever` block will be repeated over and over again.

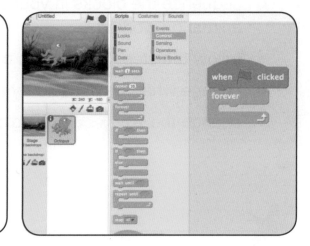

4

In the **Scripts** tab, click on **Motion** and snap a **glide...** block into the middle of the **forever** block. In the **secs** box, type **3**. In the **x** box, type **220**. In the **y** box, type **0**. Click on **Control** and snap a **wait 1 secs** block underneath the **glide...** block. Click in the **secs** box and type **0.5**.

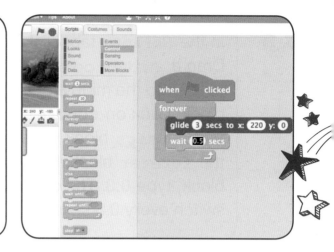

5

In the **Scripts** tab, click on **Motion** again and snap another **glide...** block into the **forever** block. In the **secs** box, type **3**. In the **x** box, type **-240**. Leave the **y** box as *0*. Click on **Control** again and snap on another **wait 1 secs** block. In the **wait...** block, type **0.5**.

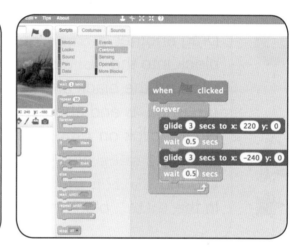

6

In the **Scripts** tab, click on **Events** again and drag a **when ⚑ clicked** block into the scripts area.

> You will create a second script using the octopus's costumes to make him look like he's swimming. He will switch between two costumes to create this effect.

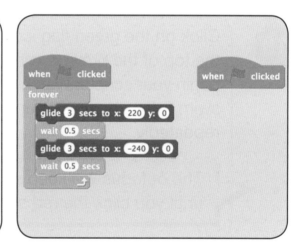

7

In the **Scripts** tab, click on **Control** and drag another **forever** block underneath your **when ⚑ clicked** block – just like you did before. Make sure they snap together.

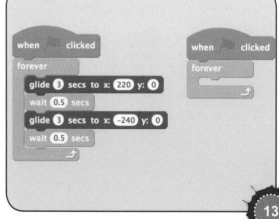

8 In the `Scripts` tab, click on `Looks`. Drag a `switch costume to...` block into the middle of the `forever` block. Click on `Control`. Snap a `wait 1 secs` block under it within the `forever` block. In the `wait...` block, type **0.3**. The costumes will switch every 0.3 seconds.

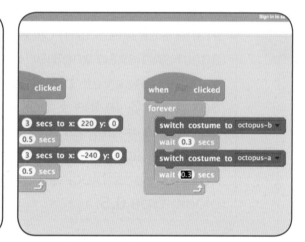

9 Drag another `switch costume to...` block into the `forever` block. Click on the black arrow next to `octopus-b` and choose `octopus-a`. Finally, click on `Control` again. Snap a `wait 1 secs` block underneath the second `switch costume to...` block. In the `wait...` block, type **0.3**.

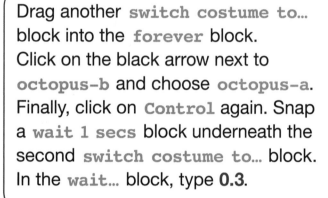

10 Click on the green flag icon at the top of the preview window to begin your scripts. Watch the octopus swim from side to side underwater repeatedly.

The octopus will keep swimming until you click the red stop icon.

You should now have something that looks like this.

Now try this . . .

- Can you select and use a different sprite and background to change the theme of your animation?

- Can you change the `wait 1 secs` or `glide...` blocks in your first script to make the octopus swim faster and slower?

- Can you change the coordinates in the `glide...` blocks so the octopus swims up and down instead of from left to right?

- Can you add in two `play sound...` blocks into the `forever` block in your first script, so the octopus makes a sound before swimming back in the other direction?

- Write instructions for a partner to perform a set of five different moves in a particular order. Only let them read it once, but challenge them to repeat the sequence three, four or five times. Can they repeat instructions in exactly the same way each time like Scratch can?

Key words

Can you explain to a partner what these words mean?

repetition   order   select   commands   sequence

How did you do?

Think about what you did in this activity. Did you:

- change the values in the `glide...` blocks so the octopus swam from left to right?

- change the `switch costume to...` blocks so the octopus moved like it was swimming?

- use the `forever` command correctly in the second script so the octopus switched between its two costumes repeatedly?

- use two `when ⚑ clicked` blocks so there were two different scripts being performed at once?

Activity 3: Scratch
Executing actions in different ways

You can program scripts to start in various ways, such as by pressing different keys on the keyboard. In this activity you will write a script to make a penguin change colour when you press the space bar.

1 Right-click on the cat and click on `delete`. Click on the `Choose sprite from library` icon and select the `Penguin2 Talk`. Click `OK`.

The penguin has two costumes which can be used to make it look like he is waving as he walks.

2 Click on the `Choose backdrop from library` icon on the bottom left and click on the `Nature` theme. Select `slopes` and then click `OK`.

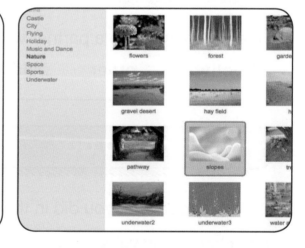

3 Click on `Penguin2 Talk` in the *Sprites* box. Now click on the `Scripts` tab and then on `Events`. Drag and drop a `when` ⚑ `clicked` block into the scripts area. In the `Scripts` tab, click on `Control` and drag and snap a `forever` block underneath the `when` ⚑ `clicked` block.

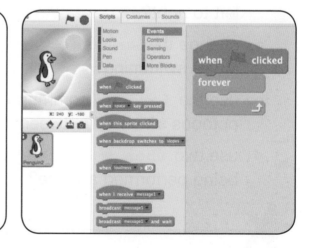

4

In the `Scripts` tab, click on `Motion` and snap a `glide...` block into the `forever` block. In the `secs` box, type **2**. In the `x` box, type **220**. Leave the `y` box as *0*. Click on `Control` and snap a `wait 1 secs` block underneath the `glide...` block.

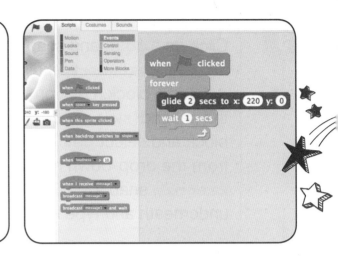

5

In the `Scripts` tab, click on `Motion` and snap another `glide...` block into the `forever` block. In the `secs` box, type **2**. In the `x` box, type **-240**. Leave the `y` box as *0*. Next click on `Control` and snap on another `wait 1 secs` block.

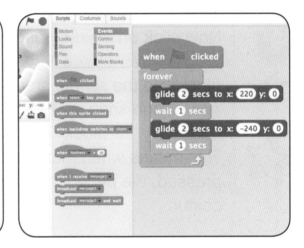

6

In the `Scripts` tab, click on `Events` and drag another `when ⚐ clicked` block into the scripts area. Next click on `Control` and drag another `forever` block underneath your `when ⚐ clicked` block – just like you did before.

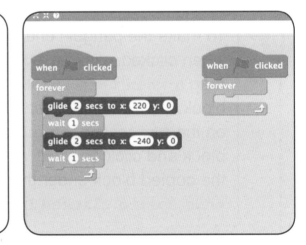

7

In the `Scripts` tab, click on `Looks`. Drag a `switch costume to...` block into the middle of the `forever` block. Click on `Control` again. Snap a `wait 1 secs` block underneath it in the `forever` block. In the `wait...` block, type **0.2**.

17

8

Click on `Looks` and snap another `switch costume to...` block into the `forever` block. Click on the arrow in the second `switch costume to...` block and select `penguin2 talk-a` from the drop-down menu. Click on `Control`, snap a `wait 1 secs` block underneath and type in **0.2**.

9

Now click on `Events` and drag and drop a `when space key pressed` block into the scripts area. Click on `Looks` and snap a `change color effect by 25` block underneath. This means when the space bar is pressed, the penguin should change colour.

10

To make the penguin change colour when clicked, click on `Events` and drag a `when this sprite clicked` block into the scripts area. Right-click on the `change color effect by 25` block and click on `duplicate`. Snap the copied block under the `when this sprite clicked` block.

11

Click on the green flag icon at the top of the preview window to run your scripts. Watch the penguin move from side to side, waving as he goes. Press the space bar and watch him change colour. He will turn a different colour each time it is pressed. Try clicking the penguin too.

Now try this . . .

- Can you change the script so that the penguin changes colour when another key is pressed instead of the space bar? Can you program other keys to have different effects on the penguin?

- Can you add another block to the `when space key pressed` script so the penguin says hello as well as changes colour when the space bar is pressed?

- Can you change the coordinates in the `glide…` blocks so the penguin walks up and down instead of from left to right?

- Can you add in a fourth script so the penguin plays a sound when the up arrow key is pressed?

 Think about how you use computers and other electronic devices. List the different types of input a user can use to make things happen apart from pressing the space bar.

Key words

Can you explain to a partner what these words mean?

input   **output**   **script**   **program**

How did you do?

Think about what you did in this activity. Did you:

- create a script that animated a penguin so he moved from side to side?

- create a script so the user could change the colour of the penguin by pressing the space bar?

- make the penguin switch costume so it looked like he was waving?

- change the script so pressing another key instead of the space bar made the penguin change colour?

Activity 4: Scratch
Using time to sequence events

You can program more than one sprite within an animation in Scratch. Use the steps below to animate a conversation between a shark and a starfish.

1

Right-click on the cat and click on `delete` to remove it. Now click on the `Choose sprite from library` icon and then click on `Animals`. Select `Shark` and click `OK`. Go back to the library and choose `Starfish`. Click `OK`.

> We need two sprites so they can talk to each other.

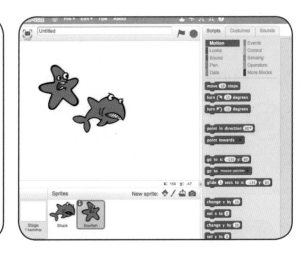

2

Click on the `Choose backdrop from library` icon and click on the `Nature` theme. Select `underwater3` and then click `OK`.

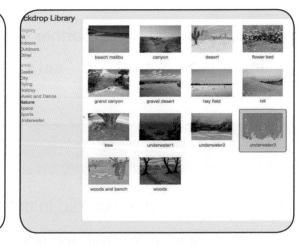

3

Select the starfish sprite in the *Sprites* box and then click on the `Scripts` tab. Click on `Events` and drag a `when clicked` block into the scripts area. Now click on `Motion` and snap a `glide…` block underneath. In the `x` box, type **180**. In the `y` box, type **0**.

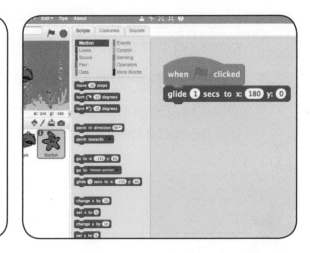

4 Click on `Looks` and drag across a `say Hello! for 2 secs` block. In the `secs` box, type **1**. Now click on `Control` and drag across a `wait 1 secs` block. Go back to `Looks` and snap on another `say...` block. In the first box, type **You look grumpy!**.

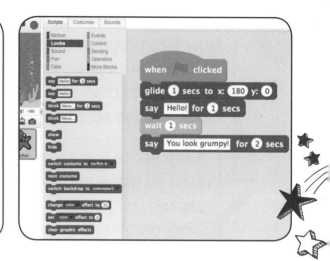

5 Go back to `Control` and drag across another `wait 1 secs` block. Then go back to `Looks` and snap a `think Hmm... for 2 secs` block on. Type **Uh oh...** in the first box. Then snap a `change color effect by 25` block underneath too.

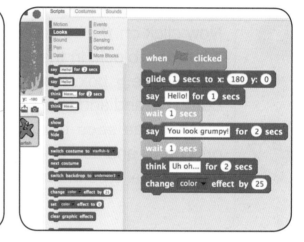

6 Click on `Control` and snap on another `wait 1 secs` block. Then go back to `Looks`. Snap on another `say...` block but this time type in the first box **I've got to go!**.

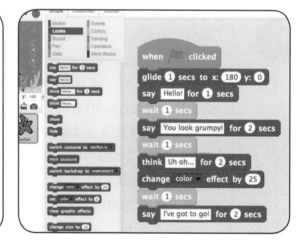

7 The starfish script is almost done! Just click on `Motion` and snap on a `glide...` block. In the `secs` box, type **0.2**. In the `x` box, type **180**. In the `y` box, type **270**. The script for the starfish is now ready. Read over it. What do you think it will do?

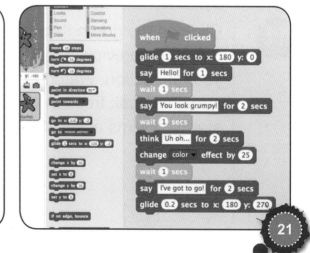

8

Now let's program the shark. Click on **Shark** in the *Sprites* box. Then click on **Events** and drag a **when ⚑ clicked** block into the scripts area.

> Each sprite has its own scripts area so make sure you have clicked on the sprite you want to work on.

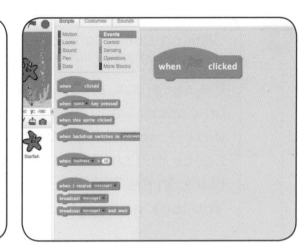

9

Now click on **Motion**. Drag across a **glide…** block. In the **x** box, type **-180**. In the **y** box, type **0**. Click on **Control** and add in a **wait 1 secs** block. In the **secs** box, type **5**. Click on **Looks** and add a **say…** block. In the first box type in **I'm hungry…**.

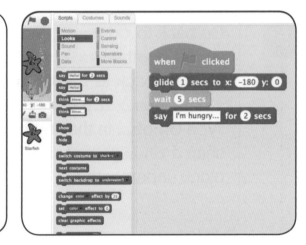

10

Click on **Control** and snap on another **wait 1 secs** block. Finally, click on **Motion** and snap on a **glide…** block. In the **secs** box, type **0.5**. In the **x** box, type **-50**. In the **y** box, type **10**. The shark is now programmed too. Can you predict what he is going to do?

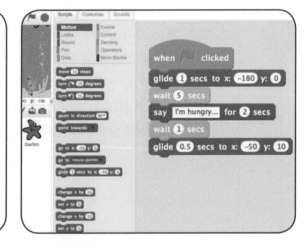

11

Click on the green flag icon ⚑ at the top of the preview window to begin your animation. Watch as the starfish and shark talk to each other and the starfish swims away at the end.

Now try this . . .

- Can you add some more `say...` and `wait...` blocks and make the conversation between the shark and starfish a bit longer?

- Can you use the `switch costume to...` block to use the other costumes both sprites have?

- Can you change the ending so the shark follows the starfish as he swims away?

- Can you add in a third sprite, perhaps a fish, for the shark and starfish to talk to?

 Can you write down two scripts that code a conversation between two friends? They can be talking about what they did at the weekend. Use the commands `wait...` and `say...` just like you did in Scratch.

Key words

Can you explain to a partner what these words mean?

sequence   **conversation**   **program**   **script**

How did you do?

Think about what you did in this activity. Did you:

- create an animation with two sprites interacting with one another?

- change the script to make the conversation longer?

- change the script to include costume switches?

- change the script so the ending of the animation changed?

- add in a third sprite?

Activity 5: PowerPoint Sequencing an animation

Sequencing is all about putting things in the right order. By sequencing images that change slightly each time, you can create an animation. Work through the activity to sequence an animation of a plant growing.

1 Open a new slideshow in PowerPoint. On the `Home` tab, click on `Layout` and then select `Blank`. This will remove all text boxes from the slide. On the `Insert` tab, click on `Shapes` and then select the rectangle tool. Click and drag to create a rectangle across the bottom of the slide.

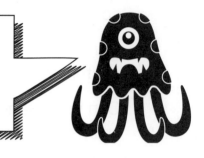

2 Right-click on the rectangle and use the `Shape Fill` colour tool to make it brown. Right-click again and select `Shape Outline`. Select `No Outline` to remove the outline. This brown rectangle will be the soil in your animation sequence. It won't change.

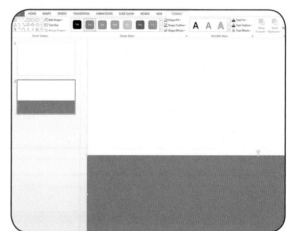

3 On the `Insert` tab, click on `Shapes` then select the oval tool (under *Basic Shapes*) to draw a seed shape just below the top of the 'soil'. Colour it light brown and remove the outline just like you did in step 2.

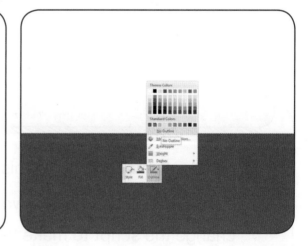

24

4 Click on the slide on the left of the screen. Right-click and select `Duplicate Slide`. Click on the second slide. On the `Insert` tab, click on `Shapes`, then under *Lines* select the *Scribble* tool. Use this to draw a green line around the seed to show the shoot.

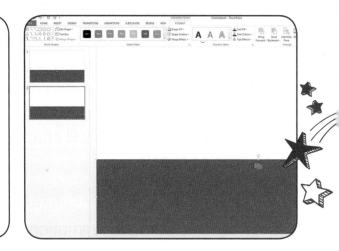

5 Now duplicate slide 2 (as in step 4) so you can change it to create the third slide. Use the *Scribble* tool again to draw a small white line coming from the seed. This shows the root starting to grow. Make the green shoot longer so it looks like a stem.

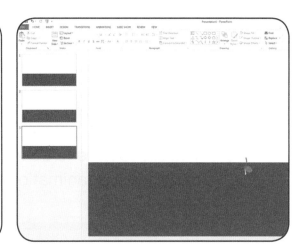

6 Duplicate slide 3. Use the *Scribble* tool to make the shoot and root a bit longer on slide 4. It will look like the roots are growing in your animation! Use the *Scribble* tool to draw a leaf coming off the stem.

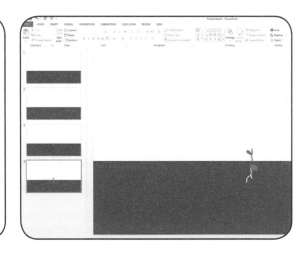

7 Now duplicate slide 4. In slide 5, use the *Scribble* tool to make the roots and stem longer. Copy and paste your leaf from slide 4. Click on the copied leaf and place your pointer on the tiny green circle to turn the leaf around. Add it to the other side of the stem.

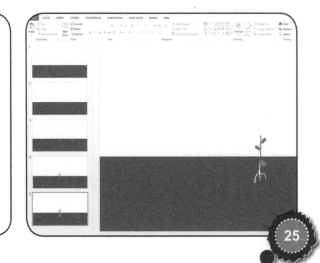

8 Duplicate slide 5. Use the *Scribble* tool to extend the roots on slide 6. Now use the *Scribble* tool to add a green bud at the top of the stem. Can you predict what you will change in the next slide?

Each slide has to change slightly to create the animation sequence.

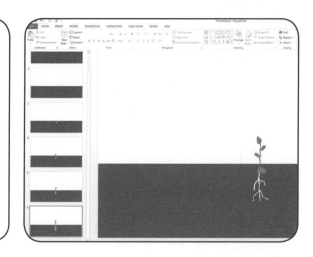

9 Duplicate slide 6. On slide 7, use the `Shape Fill` colour tool to change the bud to the petal colour you would like your flower to have.

The slides have to be in the right order for your animation to make sense.

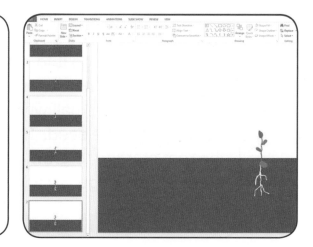

10 Duplicate slide 7. Copy and paste the flower bud several times on slide 8. Arrange the buds in a circle to create petals for your flower. Turn the petals to face different directions using the green circle tool. Add small yellow circles for the pollen. The sequence is now complete.

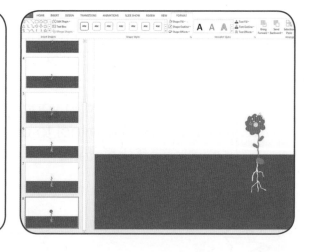

11 Click on the `Transitions` tab. Under *Advance Slide*, make sure the *After* box is ticked. Set at **00:03.00** and select `Apply To All`. Click on the `Slide Show` menu and then select `From Beginning` to watch your sequence play as an animation.

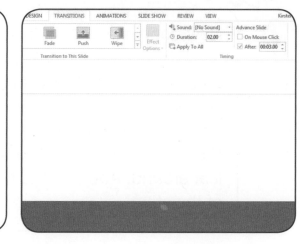

Now try this . . .

- o Can you change the speed at which your animation plays using the *Transitions* tools?

- o Can you add some sky and clouds in the background and change them slightly on each slide so it looks like they are moving when your animation plays?

- o Can you create a similar animation for a different plant or flower?

- o Can you create a sequence of slides to animate two or more flowers growing?

- Draw a sequence of pictures that show the full life cycle of a plant. Mix them up and challenge a partner to put them in order. How did they know what order to put them in?

Key words

Can you explain to a partner what these words mean?

animation   **sequence**   **change**   **duplicate**   **order**

How did you do?

Think about what you did in this activity. Did you:

- o duplicate your slides to allow you to make changes to the sequence of your animation?

- o change the picture of the flower slightly each time?

- o copy and paste different parts of your picture?

- o sequence the different drawings correctly so your animation made sense?

- o change the slide show settings so your animation played continuously?

- o change the speed at which your animation played?

- o add changes to the background in your animation?

Activity 6: PowerPoint Creating an animation on one slide

You can create animations in PowerPoint with only one slide. In this activity you will use some other sets of instructions (functions) to create an animation of bees pollinating flowers.

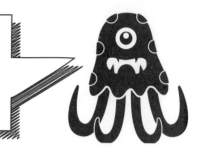

1 Open the PowerPoint file that you created in the last activity. Click on `File` and then `Save As`. Give the file a new name. Your new animation will be based on the last slide. Delete all the other slides so that only the last one is left. (Right-click each slide on the left of the screen and select `Delete Slide`.)

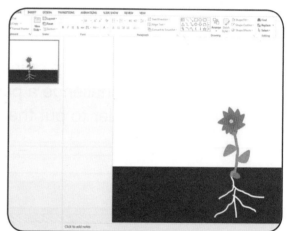

2 Now you need more flowers. Click and drag the mouse over all the objects (shapes) that make up your flower. Press the `Ctrl` and `G` keys together to group all the parts of the flower together.

3 With the flower selected, right-click on it and then click on `Copy`. Now right-click elsewhere on the slide and click on `Paste`. Another flower should appear. Do this again so you have three flowers on the slide. Move the flowers so they are spread out across the slide.

28

4

It's time to create a bee. Click on the **Insert** menu and then the **Shapes** menu. Use the oval tool to create three ovals: one for the bee's body, one for its eye and one for wings. Highlight and group together the whole bee (see step 2) and copy and paste so you have three bees.

5

Now you will animate each bee to enter the slide in a different way, one after the other. Click on the bee on the left. Then click on the **Animations** menu and **Fly In**. Now click on **Effect Options** and **From Left**. This means that the bee will fly in from the left.

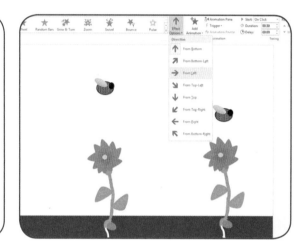

6

Click on the middle bee and set it to fly in too. Click on **Effect Options**. This time, choose **From Top-Right**. Click on the **Start** menu (at the top right of your screen) and select **After Previous**. The animation for the second bee will only start after the first bee has finished moving.

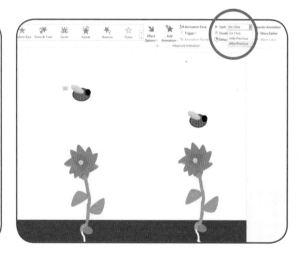

7

To animate the last bee's entrance, click on the last bee, then on **Fly In**. Click **From Bottom-Left** in the **Effects Options**. Again, choose **After Previous** so it happens after the second bee's animation has finished. Try changing the duration to **01.00** so the bee flies in slower.

29

8 Let's add one final animation to the last bee. Click on it again and then on **Add Animation**. Select **Spin** under *Emphasis* and set it to start **After Previous** as before. This means once all the bees have entered, it will spin on the spot.

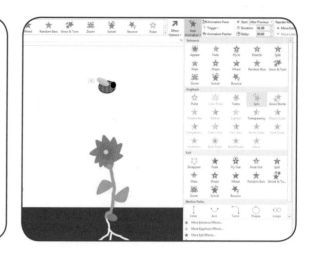

9 Now it's time to make the bees move around the flowers. Click on the first bee and then on **Add Animation**. Under the *Motion Paths* menu select **Custom Path**. Using the mouse, draw a path from the bee to the first flower. Make sure you double-click when done. Set it to start **After Previous**.

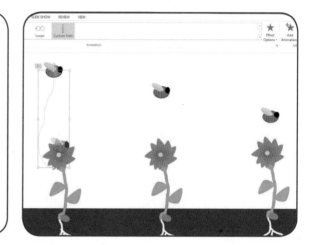

10 Repeat the step above for the other two bees. Set these two to start **With Previous**.

> This means all the bees will start following their motion paths together.

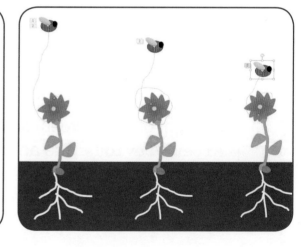

11 With all the animations set, it's time to view your animation. Click on the **Slide Show** menu, and then select **From Beginning**. Watch carefully as the three bees enter the animation in order, and the last one spins around, before all three fly to the flowers.

> Check your *Transitions* settings as for step 11 of activity 5.

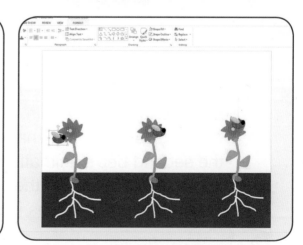

Now try this . . .

- Can you change the speed at which the bees move by changing the custom motion path settings?

- Can you change the order in which the different animations happen?

- Can you add some more bees? Can you animate them to fly between different flowers?

- Can you use different animation functions to find some other ways for the bees to enter the animation?

 Create a storyboard (a sequence of images in order) for a new animation that uses the functions you have learned about in this activity. Your new animation can be about anything you like!

Key words

Can you explain to a partner what these words mean?

animation   **order**   **motion path**   **sequence**   **function**   **instructions**

How did you do?

Think about what you did in this activity. Did you:

- create an animation of bees pollinating flowers using one PowerPoint slide?

- change the speed at which the bees moved?

- change the order in which the different animations happened?

- animate some more bees to move between the flowers?

- change the way the bees entered the animation?

- create a storyboard for a new animation?

Activity 7: PowerPoint Creating an interactive animation

We can use coding to make parts of animations interactive, so a user can click the mouse (input) to control what happens on screen (the output). In this activity you will use triggers to create an interactive animation.

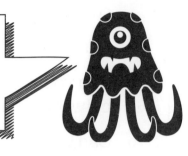

1 Start by opening the PowerPoint file you made in the last activity. Use `Save As` to save it under a new name. Delete all the bees. Make the sky blue by right-clicking and selecting `Format Background`…. Under *Fill*, select `Solid fill` and light blue.

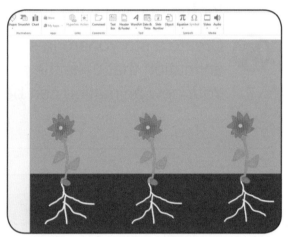

2 To create the sun, use the oval tool and the `Shift` key to draw two circles, one a bit bigger than the other. Make the smaller one orange and the larger one yellow.

> To make a circle, hold down the `Shift` key with the oval tool.

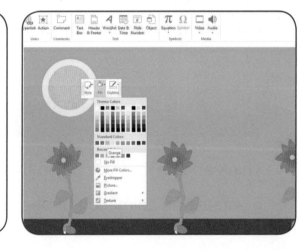

3 Click on the bigger yellow circle, then click on the `Animations` menu and select the `Grow/Shrink` option. This will make the yellow circle grow and shrink.

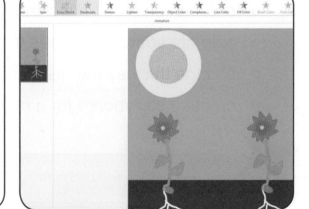

4

Click on the `Triggers` button. Select `On Click of` and choose the name of the yellow circle from the list (it will be `Oval...`).

Setting this trigger means the sun animation will only start when the user clicks on the yellow circle.

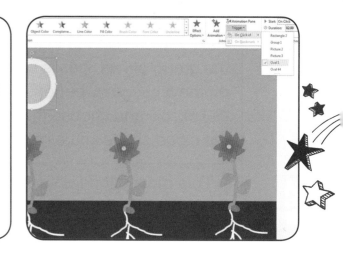

5

Plants also need water to grow, so let's create rain clouds. Click on `Insert` and then `Shapes`. Use the cloud tool (under *Basic Shapes*) to draw a cloud shape in the sky.

You could experiment with different shadow and shape effects.

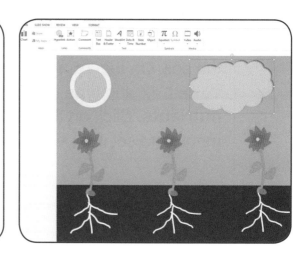

6

Let's make rain fall from your cloud. Use the line tool to draw a diagonal line. Right-click the line and select `Format Shape...`. Click on `Line Style` and change the dash type. Select `Line Color` and make it blue. Copy and paste the line a few times.

7

Click and drag the mouse over all the rain lines to select them all. Now press `Ctrl` and `G` together to group them so you can treat them as one object. Then click on the `Animations` menu, select `More Exit Effects...` and then `Dissolve Out`.

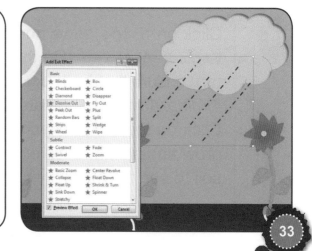

8

Next you can set the triggers. While the group of rain lines is selected, click on the `Triggers` button. Select `On Click of` and choose the name of the cloud shape in the menu.

> This means the rain will be animated when the user clicks on the cloud.

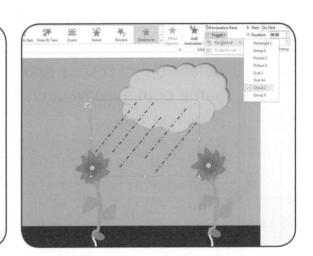

9

A plant also needs nutrients from the soil. On the `Insert` tab, select `Text Box` and type in the word **nutrients**. Click on the `Animations` menu and set it to `Appear`.

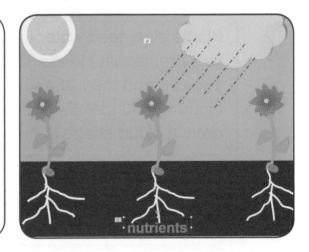

10

Now set a trigger for this text so it only appears when the user clicks on the soil. Click on the `Triggers` button and select `On Click of` and choose the name of the brown rectangle in the list.

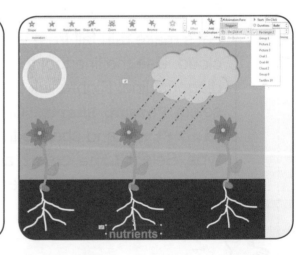

11

Click on `Slide Show` and select `From Beginning`. (On the *Transitions* tab, ensure that both boxes under *Timing/Advance Slide* are unclicked.) Click on the sun to watch the rays grow and shrink. Click on the rain and soil to see the other animations.

Now try this . . .

- Can you change the speed at which the sun's rays grow and shrink by changing the custom animation effect settings?

- Can you use a different custom animation effect to make the rain appear?

- Can you change the custom animation effect repeat settings so the rain keeps falling and doesn't stop after one click?

- Can you change the custom animation effect settings so the rain appears as soon as the sun animation is over? Maybe a rainbow could appear after both are finished?

 What other devices can you think of that are operated by a user clicking or pressing a button? How many can you think of? Think about devices in school and at home.

Key words

Can you explain to a partner what these words mean?

animation   **trigger**   **input**   **output**

How did you do?

Think about what you did in this activity. Did you:

- create an interactive animation on one slide?

- change the speed of the sun animation?

- try out different animation settings on the raindrops?

- change the settings so the rain didn't stop after the cloud was clicked?

- change the settings so the rain appeared as soon as the sun animation finished, followed by a rainbow?

Activity 8: PowerPoint Using hyperlinks in slides

Many PowerPoints are linear: the slides always play one after another. Hyperlinks let the user choose which slide comes next. In this activity you will create a slideshow that allows users to build their own flower.

1

Open a new slideshow in PowerPoint. Start by right-clicking on the slide and clicking on `Layout`. Click on `Title Only`. Click in the title box and type the first question: **Do you want pointed or round petals?**

> Each slide will ask the user a question to help them design their flower.

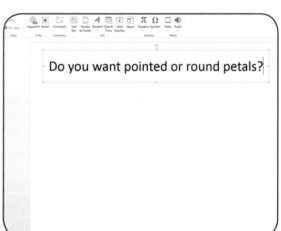

2

Now click on the `Insert` menu and then `Table`. Draw a table with two columns and one row. Click inside the first cell and type **Pointed**. Click in the second cell and type **Round**. Click on the slide in the *Slides* tab. Right-click and select `Duplicate Slide` to make a second slide.

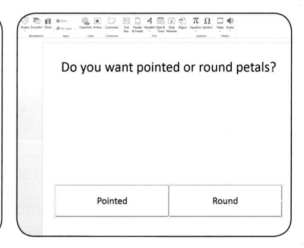

3

Click in the top text box and change the question to **What colour pointed petals?** Now right-click in one of the table cells and then on `Insert` and `Insert Columns to the Right` so there are three cells. Replace the text by typing **Red**, **Yellow** and **Pink** in the cells.

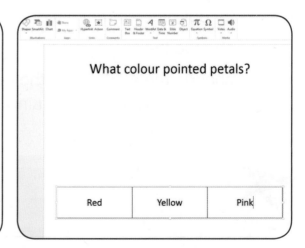

4

Now duplicate slide 2. Click in the top text box and change the word *pointed* to **round**.

Can you change the colour of the *Red*, *Yellow* and *Pink* cells to match their labels to make it easier for the user to use?

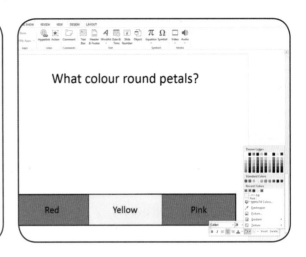

5

On the `Home` tab, click on `New Slide`. Click in the top text box. Type **Here's your flower!**. Press `Enter` then type **Pointed red petals**. On the `Insert` tab, click on `Shapes` and select the 8-point star. Click on `Shape Fill` and choose red. Use the oval tool to make an orange circle.

6

Duplicate slide 4. Click in the text box and change *red* to **yellow**. Click on the flower and then the `Shape Fill` icon. Click on yellow to change the colour of the flower. Now duplicate slide 5. In the new slide (6) change the word *yellow* to **pink** and the flower colour to pink.

7

Duplicate slide 6. Click in the text box. Change *Pointed* to **Round** and *pink* to **red**. Delete the flower. Use the oval tool to draw four ovals. Right-click on `Shape Fill` to make them red. Use the oval tool while pressing the `Shift` key to draw a circle. Colour it orange.

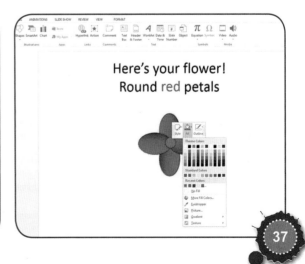

8 Duplicate slide 7. Click in the text box. Change *red* to **yellow**. Click on each petal while pressing the `Shift` key to select them all. Click on the `Shape Fill` icon and click on yellow. Duplicate slide 8 and change the word *yellow* to **pink** and make the flower pink.

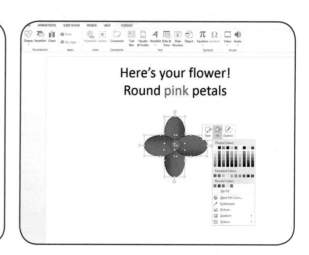

9 Now let's hyperlink the slides together to allow the user to select the next slide. Go to slide 1. Highlight the word *Pointed*. Right-click then click `Hyperlink`. Click on `Place in This Document`. Click on `slide 2` and `OK`. Repeat with the word *Round* but hyperlink to `slide 3`.

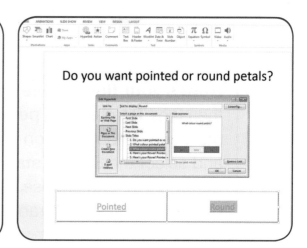

10 Go to slide 2. Hyperlink the word *Red* to `slide 4`. Hyperlink the word *Yellow* to `slide 5` and the word *Pink* to `slide 6`. Finally, go to slide 3. Hyperlink the word *Red* to `slide 7`. Hyperlink *Yellow* to `slide 8` and *Pink* to `slide 9`.

> Hyperlinking lets the user go to a specific chosen slide, not just the next one in the sequence.

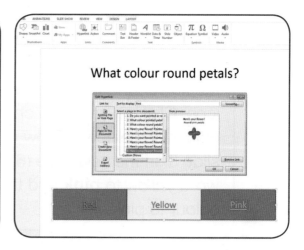

11 To test your animation, click on the `Slide Show` tab and then select `From Beginning`. Read the questions and click on answers to design your own flower. If something doesn't link as it should, you will need to do some debugging and fix the problem.

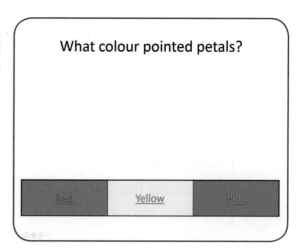

Now try this . . .

- Can you change the colour of the red petals to purple? Which other slides will you need to change?

- Can you add a button on each *Here's your flower!* slide to take you back to the first slide once you are done?

- Can you add a fourth petal colour and change the slides and hyperlinks to allow users to create a different-coloured flower?

- Can you add in a third petal type and change the slides and hyperlinks to allow users to create a different-shaped flower?

 Draw a tree diagram for someone to follow to design their own T-shirt with options for different colours and different sleeve lengths (long and short). What about a tree diagram for something completely different?

Key words

Can you explain to a partner what these words mean?

sequence   **hyperlink**   **option**   **user**   **debug**

How did you do?

Think about what you did in this activity. Did you:

- create a slide show that allows the user to design their own flower?

- change the petal colour from red to purple and change any other related slides?

- add a button to each *Here's your flower!* slide that takes a user back to the first slide?

- add a fourth petal colour and change the slides and hyperlinks to allow users to create a different-coloured flower?

- add a third petal type and change the slides and hyperlinks to allow users to create a different-shaped flower?

Activity 9: Excel Using the random function

If you had to throw a die 100 times and record all the different scores, it would take a very long time! You are going to simulate throwing a die 100 times at the press of a button.

1 Start by clicking on cell A1. Type the word **Scores**. Press the **Enter** key.

All the cells in Excel are labelled according to what column and row they are in. The letter tells you the column and the number tells you the row.

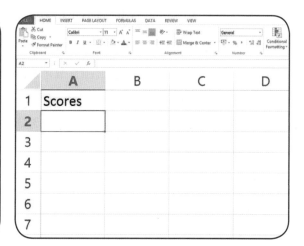

2 Click on cell A2 and type in **=RANDBETWEEN(1,6)**. Now press the **Enter** key. A number between 1 and 6 is now in cell A2.

This function tells Excel to randomly choose any number between 1 and 6.

3 Click on cell A2 again then click at the end of the function in the white box above the cells (the formula bar). Press the **Enter** key. A new random number between 1 and 6 appears each time you repeat these three actions. (On some computers you can simply press **F9** to do this.)

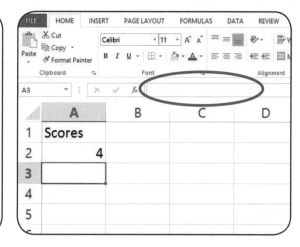

4 You have simulated one throw so far, but we want to simulate 100 throws. This means copying the random function code into 99 more cells. Start by clicking on cell A2 so it is highlighted with the box around it.

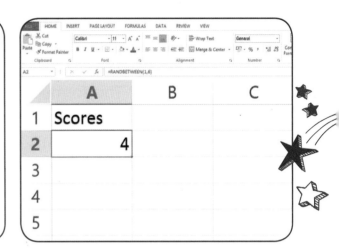

5 Next move the pointer on to the small square at the bottom right of cell A2.

The pointer will turn from a white cross to a black cross when you hover over the black square.

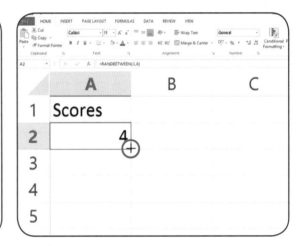

6 Click on the square and drag the box downwards to cell A11. Then release it. Next click on the square and drag the box across to J11. Each cell from A2 to J11 should contain a randomly generated dice throw. You now have the scores of 100 random die throws.

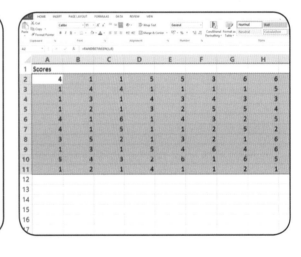

7 Cells A2–J11 should now be highlighted. Click at the end of the function in the formula bar above the cells. Press the **Enter** key to run the random function in all the cells again (or press **F9**). This simulates throwing 100 dice at the press of just one button!

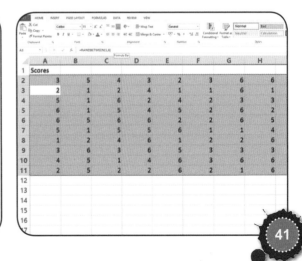

8

Remember when you typed in *=RANDBETWEEN(1,6)* at the start of the activity? This formula is a piece of code that tells the computer to pick a random number from 1 to 6. Each time you press **Enter**, the computer reads the code and generates the random numbers.

	A	B	C	D
2	=RANDBETWEEN(1,6)			
3	3	4	5	
4	6	1	5	
5	6	6	4	
6	1	1	6	
7	3	2	5	
8	5	3	4	

9

You will need this Excel spreadsheet for the next activity so remember to click on **File** and then **Save** to save your virtual die.

If you want to try any of the activities in *Now try this...*, make sure you use **Save As** to create a new file.

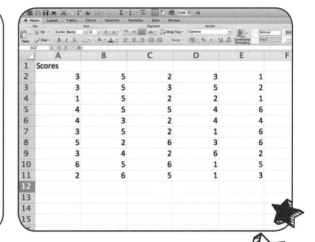

	A	B	C	D	E	F
1	Scores					
2	3	5	2	3	1	
3	3	5	3	5	2	
4	1	5	2	2	1	
5	4	5	5	4	6	
6	4	3	2	4	4	
7	3	5	2	1	6	
8	5	2	6	3	6	
9	3	4	2	6	2	
10	6	5	6	1	5	
11	2	6	5	1	3	
12						
13						
14						
15						

Now try this . . .

- o Can you change the numbers in the random function so it generates a number between 1 and 10 instead of 1 and 6?

- o Can you simulate 200 die throws instead of 100?

- o Can you simulate throwing two dice by changing the formula to *RANDBETWEEN(1,6) + RANDBETWEEN(1,6)*?

- o Can you simulate three dice at once and use a formula to work out their totals?

 What other tasks could we simulate by writing code for a computer to read?

Key words

Can you explain to a partner what these words mean?

cell   **function**   **formula**   **simulate**   **random**

How did you do?

Think about what you did in this activity. Did you:

- o simulate throwing a die 100 times?

- o generate numbers between 1 and 10?

- o copy the function into more cells to simulate 200 die throws instead of 100?

- o simulate two dice being thrown?

- o simulate throwing three dice at the press of a key?

Activity 10: Excel Using conditional formatting

Now you have created a spreadsheet that simulates 100 die rolls, you are going to use Excel to highlight each of the different numbers in a different colour so you can quickly see which numbers have been 'rolled' the most.

1 Start by opening the Excel file from the last activity. Click on cell A2 so it has a box around it. Drag the box down to cell A11, release it and then drag it and across to J11. All the die scores should now be highlighted.

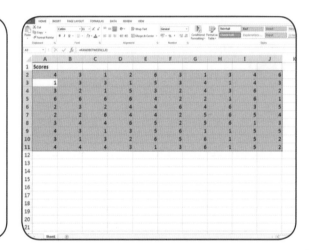

2 Click on the `Conditional Formatting` box at the top of the screen (in the middle). Then click on `Highlight Cells Rules` in the menu. Next click on `Equal To...` in the new menu that appears.

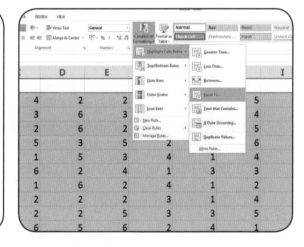

3 In the `Equal To...` box, click on the first white box and type **1**. Click on the arrow in the second box and then on `Custom Format`....

You are going to use selection here by telling Excel that if the score is 1, then colour the cell purple.

4

Now you can see the *Format Cells* box. Click on the **Fill** tab at the top. Click on purple in the colour palette. Then click **OK**. Finally, click **OK** on the **Equal To...** box. Look at your die scores. All the scores of 1 should now be purple.

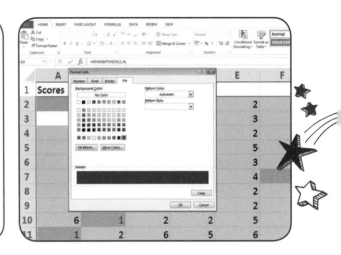

5

Highlight cells A2–J11 again. Click on **Conditional Formatting**, then **Highlight Cells Rules** and **Equal To...** as in step 2. In the first box, type **2**. In the second box menu, click on **Custom Format...**. Click on dark blue, then **OK** and **OK** again. All 2 scores should be dark blue.

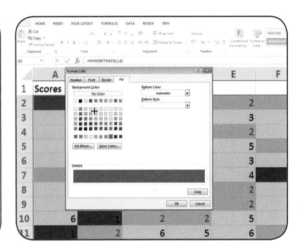

6

Now let's set a rule to colour all scores of 3 green. Click **Conditional Formatting**, then **Highlight Cells Rules** and **Equal To...**. In the first box, type **3**. In the second box menu, click on **Custom Format...**. Click on green and click **OK**. Then click **OK** again.

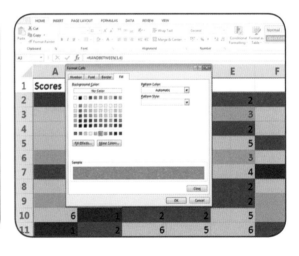

7

Click on **Conditional Formatting** again, then **Highlight Cells Rules** and **Equal To...** again. In the first box, type **4**. In the second box menu, click on **Custom Format...**. Click on yellow and click **OK**. Then click **OK** again.

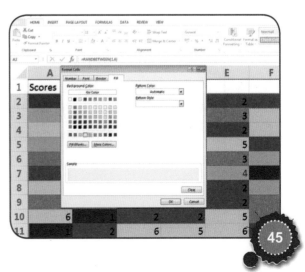

8 Click on **Conditional Formatting**, then **Highlight Cells Rules** and **Equal To…** once more. In the first box, type **5**. In the second box menu, click on **Custom Format….** Click on orange and click **OK**. Then click **OK** again.

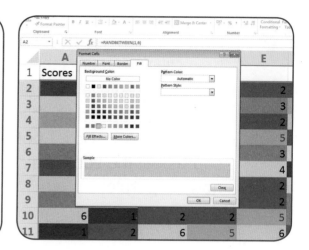

9 Click on **Conditional Formatting**, then **Highlight Cells Rules** and **Equal To…** for one last time. In the first box, type **6**. In the second box menu, click on **Custom Format….** Click on red and click **OK**. Then click **OK** again.

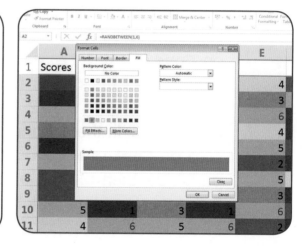

10 All the scores should now be colour-coded. We have told Excel to select different colours depending on the number in the cell.

11 With all the scores highlighted, put your pointer at the end of the function in the formula bar and press **Enter** again (or press **F9**). As the scores change, watch their colours change too. Click on **File** and then **Save**.

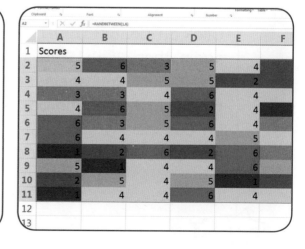

Now try this . . .

- Can you adjust the conditional formatting rules so a score of 4 is highlighted light blue instead of yellow?

- Can you create conditional formatting rules so the text changes colour rather than the fill colour of the cell?

- Can you add another conditional formatting rule so all scores of 6 have white text?

- Can you create a rule so scores of 3 or less are coloured red?

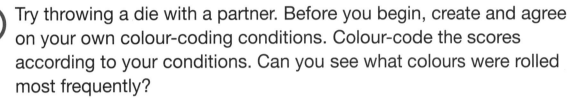 Try throwing a die with a partner. Before you begin, create and agree on your own colour-coding conditions. Colour-code the scores according to your conditions. Can you see what colours were rolled most frequently?

Key words

Can you explain to a partner what these words mean?

cell   **function**   **condition**   **conditional formatting**   **rule**

How did you do?

Think about what you did in this activity. Did you:

- follow the steps to colour-code the 100 die throws depending on the score?

- adjust the conditional formatting so scores of 4 were coloured light blue instead of yellow?

- create conditional formatting rules to colour the text instead of the fill colour of the cells?

- add another conditional formatting rule so scores of 6 had white text?

- create a rule so scores of 3 or less were coloured red?

Activity 11: Excel
Using functions to analyse data

In this activity you are going to use Excel to find out different information about the 100 die throws. We call this analysing data.

1 Start by opening the Excel file from the last activity. Click on cell L1. Type the word **Total**. Then press the `Enter` key.

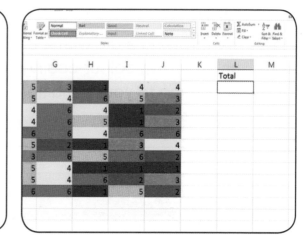

2 Now click on cell L2. Type in **=SUM(A2:J11)** and press `Enter`. The number that has appeared in cell L2 is the total of all the 100 die scores added together. How long would this take you to add them all up?

3 Click on cell A2 and put your mouse pointer at the end of the function in the formula bar. Press `Enter` to generate 100 new die throws. Look carefully at the *Total* number (in L2). It should change as the 100 die scores change.

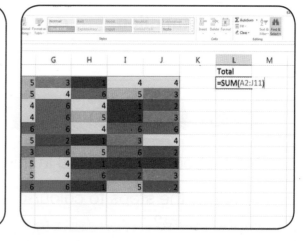

On some computers you can use `F9` to run the function again.

4

Next click on cell L4 and type in **Average**. Press `Enter`.

The average score is all the scores added up and then divided by the total number of scores (100).

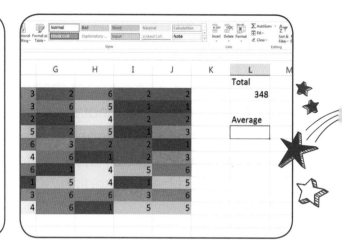

5

Click on cell L5. Type in **=L2/100** and press `Enter`. The number that appears in cell L5 is the average of all the 100 die scores.

6

Again, put your mouse pointer at the end of the function in the formula bar and press `Enter` (or try pressing the `F9` key) a few times to generate 100 new die throw scores. Watch as the average changes each time you press `Enter` or `F9`.

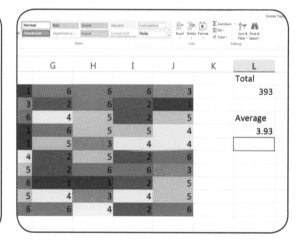

7

Next click on cell L7. Type in **Median**. Then press `Enter`.

The median is the score that would be in the middle of the list if all 100 scores were ordered in a list from smallest to biggest.

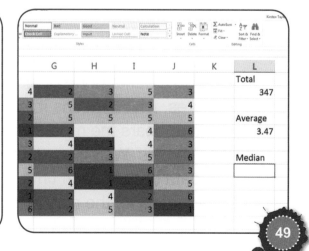

8 Click on cell L8. Type in =**MEDIAN(A2:J11)** and press **Enter**. The number that appears in cell L8 is the median of all the 100 die scores. If you wrote all the 100 die throws in order, the middle number would be the median.

9 Generate a few more die throws (select L8 and press **Enter** in the formula bar, or press **F9**). Watch the median change as the die scores change.

10 Next click on cell L10. Type in **Mode**. Then press **Enter**. Click on cell L11.

11 Type in =**MODE(A2:J11)** and press **Enter**. The number that appears in cell L11 is the mode of all the 100 die scores, which means it is the score that appears the most. Simulate more die throws. Watch as all four pieces of data update each time. What do you notice as the numbers change?

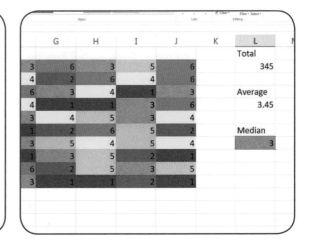

Now try this . . .

- ○ Can you change the SUM function so it only adds up the first 50 die throws? What about the final 50 throws?

- ○ Can you add in another AVERAGE function that calculates the average of the first 10 and last 10 scores? How do the two compare?

- ○ Can you calculate the minimum and maximum scores each time by using the formulas *MIN(A2:J11)* and *MAX(A2:J11)*?

 Throw a die 11 times and record the scores. Now write an algorithm for a partner explaining how to calculate the median of the 11 scores.

Key words

Can you explain to a partner what these words mean?

cell   **function**   **data**   **calculate**   **generate**

How did you do?

Think about what you did in this activity. Did you:

- ○ create functions for Excel to calculate the total, median and mode of 100 die throws?

- ○ change the SUM function so it only added up the first 50 throws?

- ○ change the SUM function again so it added up the final 50 throws?

- ○ add in two more AVERAGE functions to compare the average of the first 10 and final 10 throws?

- ○ use the MAX and MIN functions to calculate the minimum and maximum score of the 100 throws?

Activity 12: Excel Using the COUNTIF function and making a bar chart

Now let's use tables and graphs to see exactly how many of each score is thrown by creating a frequency table and graph of the results of 100 virtual die throws.

1 Start by opening the Excel file from the last activity. Click on cell N1. Type the word **Score**. Then press the Enter key. Type **Frequency** into cell O1. Press Enter.

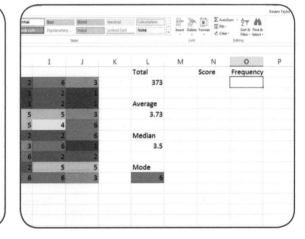

2 Now type **1** into cell N2 and press Enter. Then **2** into N3. Then type **3** in the cell under that, **4** under that, followed by **5** and **6**. Don't forget to press Enter each time.

You are going to create a frequency table to show how often each die score appears in the 100 throws.

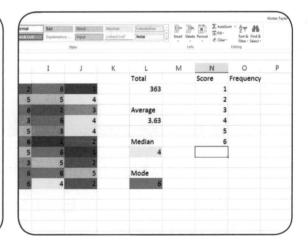

3 Click on cell O2. Type in **=COUNTIF(A2:J11,1)**. Press Enter.

This function tells Excel that 'if there is a score of 1 in cells A2 to J11, then count it'. This number is a variable because it will change each time 100 new scores are generated.

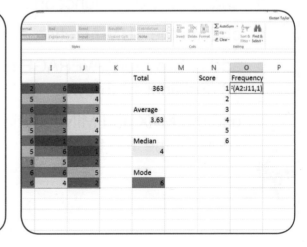

4

Click on cell O3. Type in
=**COUNTIF(A2:J11,2)**. Press Enter.

> The number that appears in cell
> O3 is the number of scores out of
> the 100 throws that are 2.

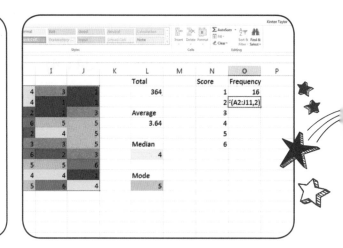

5

Click on cell O4. Type in
=**COUNTIF(A2:J11,3)**. Press Enter.
What do you think we are asking
Excel to do here? Can you predict
what we'll do next?

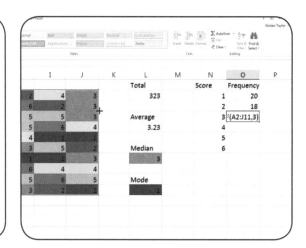

6

Click on cell O5. Type in
=**COUNTIF(A2:J11,4)**. Press Enter.

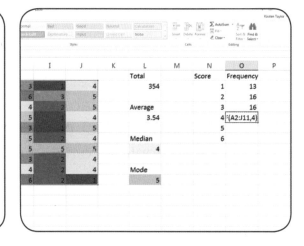

7

Click on cell O6. Type in
=**COUNTIF(A2:J11,5)**. Press Enter.

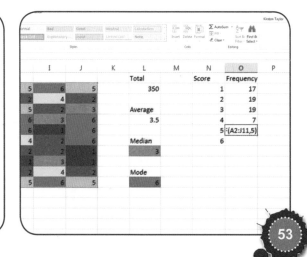

8 Click on cell O7. Type in
=COUNTIF(A2:J11,6). Press `Enter`.

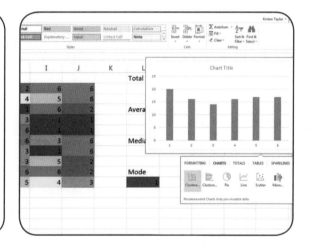

9 Now select O2 and place your pointer in the formula box. Press `Enter` to generate another 100 die throws each time (or try pressing `F9`).

> The score with the highest frequency should also be the *Mode* score (the number that appears the most times).

10 Now click on cell O2. Hold down the `Shift` key and click on cell O7 to highlight all the cells in-between. Click on the `Insert` tab at the top of your screen and select `Column`. Choose the first option from `2-D Column` `(Clustered Column)`. This will turn the data in these cells into a bar graph.

11 As well as the frequency table, you now have a bar graph showing the scores from the latest 100 throws. Press `Enter` or `F9` to update the data, as a new 100 throws are generated.

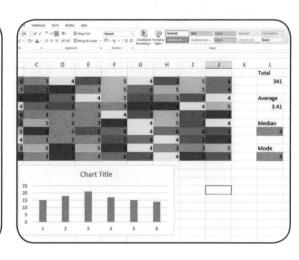

Now try this . . .

- Can you add titles to the two axes of the graph such as *Score* and *Frequency of throws*?

- Can you use conditional formatting so the colour of the bars in the graph match the colour of the cells used in activity 10?

- Can you use conditional formatting so any scores that are thrown more than 20 times are highlighted red in the frequency table?

 Record the scores of 10 die throws and draw a graph by hand. What are the benefits of drawing graphs in Excel?

Key words

Can you explain to a partner what these words mean?

cell   count   function   data   calculate   generate   chart

How did you do?

Think about what you did in this activity. Did you:

- use the COUNTIF function to create a frequency table and then create a bar chart of the data in it?

- add a title to the graph?

- label the axes?

- apply conditional formatting to the bar graph so it matched the colour-coding in activity 10?

- apply conditional formatting to the frequency table to highlight when a number was thrown more than 20 times?

Glossary

- **Animation:** a moving picture.

- **Calculate:** use addition, subtraction, multiplication and division to solve a maths question.

- **Cell:** a 'box' or container in which you can put a number.

- **Change:** add to or edit a script to produce a different outcome.

- **Chart:** a picture version of data, e.g. bar charts, pie charts and line graphs.

- **Command:** an instruction given to an object or character to make something happen.

- **Condition:** something that is true or false. E.g. number 6 is in the box. True or False?

- **Conversation:** two or more different characters talking to each other.

- **Count:** find the total number of something.

- **Data:** information that can be stored, collected or changed.

- **Duplicate:** to make a copy.

- **Formatting:** to change the style of text, e.g. alignment, spacing and bold.

- **Formula:** a maths calculation. In Excel, a formula always begins with an equals (=) sign.

- **Function:** a section of code that makes something happen.

- **Generate:** to produce something.

- **Hyperlink:** a link that takes a user to another document or web page, or to another part of a document.

- **Input:** information given to a computer to make something happen, e.g. a mouse click or button press.

- **Instruction:** telling something or someone what to do, e.g. move forward one step.

- **Motion path:** this allows you to create a 'journey' for an object so it looks like it is moving.

- **Option:** a choice to be made.

- **Order:** the sequence in which commands are processed.

- **Output:** something that a computer produces when given an instruction, e.g. an on-screen image, a sound or vibration.

- **Program:**
  1. a sequence of instructions to perform a task or solve a problem, using a programming language (noun)
  2. to create or change a program (verb).

- **Random:** not in a particular order.

- **Repetition:** the act of repeating something: following an instruction again (and again).

- **Rule:** an instruction that has to be followed.

- **Script:** a set of commands that are followed by a program.

- **Select:** to choose something.

- **Sequence:** a set of commands that are performed one after another.

- **Simulate:** use a computer to produce a 'model' of something happening, without actually having to do it.

- **Sprite:** an object or character that can be programmed.

- **Trigger:** how something is started.

- **User:** the person who uses something.